101 Things®
To Do With
Cheese

101 Things® To Do With Cheese

BY MELISSA BARLOW AND JENNIFER ADAMS

GIBBS SMITH
TO ENRICH AND INSPIRE HUMANKIND

First Edition
14 13 12 11 10   10 9 8 7 6 5 4 3 2 1

Published by
Gibbs Smith
P.O. Box 667
Layton, Utah 84041

1.800.835.4993 orders
www.gibbs-smith.com

Contributing editor: Stephanie Ashcraft
Printed and bound in Korea
Gibbs Smith books are printed on either recycled, 100% post-
consumer waste or on FSC-certified papers or on paper produced
from a 100% certified sustainable forest/controlled wood source.

Library of Congress Cataloging-in-Publication Data

101 things to do with cheese / Melissa Barlow and Jennifer Adams. — 1st ed.
    p. cm.
  ISBN-13: 978-1-4236-0649-9
  ISBN-10: 1-4236-0649-3
  1. Cookery (Cheese) I. Barlow, Melissa. II. Adams, Jennifer. III.
Title. IV. Title: One hundred one things to do with cheese.
  TX759.B36 2010
  641.6'73—dc22
                          2010008660

For my sweet little Izzie—thanks for
all the smiles. I love you! —MB

For Charlene Maynard,
my Aunt Char, one of a kind. —JA

CONTENTS

• *Southwest Layered Salad 60* • *Cheesy Broccoli and Bacon Salad 61* • *Greek Salad 62* • *Caprese Salad 63* • *Tortellini Pasta Salad 64* • *Feta Pasta Salad 65* • *Ham, Swiss, and Artichoke Pasta Salad 66* • *Three-Cheese Baked Potato Salad 67* • *Gorgonzola Potato Salad 68*

Breads & Sides

Cheesy Garlic Bread 70 • *Gooey Onion-Olive Bread 71* • *Cheddar Garlic Biscuits 72* • *Italian Biscuit Bites 73* • *Dill and Cheddar Scones 74* • *Parmesan Garlic Breadsticks 75* • *Spicy Cornbread 76* • *Asiago Mashed Potatoes 77* • *Easy Cheesy Spinach Risotto 78* • *Baked Cauliflower 79* • *Layered Potato Casserole 80* • *Creamy and Cheesy Pan Potatoes 81* • *Three-Cheese Mashed Potatoes 82*

Pizza & Pastas

Chicken Pesto Pizza 84 • *BBQ Chicken Pizza 85* • *Goat Cheese and Sun-Dried Tomato Pizza 86* • *Chicken Caesar Salad Pizza 87* • *Mexican Pizza 88* • *Artichoke Pizza 89* • *Good Ol' Mac & Cheese 90* • *Cordon Bleu Bake 91* • *Chicken Fettucine 92* • *Pesto Shrimp Pasta 93* • *Swiss Stroganoff 94* • *Gooey Lasagna 95* • *Smokey Pasta Bake 96*

Main Dishes

Chicken, Cheese, and Rice Casserole 98 • *Chicken Divan 99* • *Swiss Chicken 100* • *Rosemary Chicken 101* • *Steak with Gorgonzola Butter 102* • *Saucy Garlic and Blue Cheese Burgers 103* • *Jalapeño Turkey Burgers 104* • *Provolone Meatball Subs 105* • *Philly Cheese Steak 106* • *Fried Cheese Steaks 107* • *Cheese Enchiladas 108* • *Enchilada Casserole 109*

Desserts

Strawberry Cream Cheese Sheet Cake 112 • *Spice Cake with Creamy Frosting 113* • *Sour Cream Cheesecake 114* • *Frozen Peppermint Cheesecake 115* • *Lemon Cheesecake Bars 116* • *Cottage Cheese Raspberry Pie 117* • *Pound Cake with Mascarpone Cream 118* • *Easy Tiramisu 119* • *Ricotta Cookies 120* • *Cheddar Apple Cobbler 121* • *Cream Cheese Brownies 122*

HELPFUL HINTS

1. Many of the cheeses used in these recipes are interchangeable. If you don't like a cheese or can't find one, just use a different kind.

2. To easily cut or grate soft cheese like mozzarella, leave it in the refrigerator until just before you need it.

3. To easily cut or grate hard cheese like Parmesan, let it come to room temperature first.

4. Throw leftover cheese rinds into meatless soups for a big punch of flavor. Just make sure to pull the rind out before serving.

5. It takes refrigerated cream cheese about 1 hour before it comes to room temperature.

6. If you don't have time to let cream cheese come to room temperature, just soften in the microwave for about 25 to 30 seconds.

7. Store grated cheese in 2-cup increments in the freezer for easy use.

8. Do not freeze blocks of cheese—it changes the texture.

9. To melt cheese, bring to room temperature first. Then melt over a low heat and stir to help prevent separating.

10. Spray box graters with a touch of nonstick spray before grating to prevent cheese from sticking.

11. To prevent mold, wrap cheese in a clean cloth and refrigerate. Try dampening the cloth with a bit of salt water as well.

12. Baked cheesecakes freeze well. Just make sure to cool completely and then wrap multiple times with heavy-duty foil or with plastic wrap.

BREAKFASTS

STUFFED FRENCH TOAST

8 slices	**bread**
I container (8 ounces)	**cheesecake-flavored cream cheese spread**
I container	**fresh raspberries or 4 tablespoons raspberry jam***
2	**eggs**
¹/₂ cup	**milk**
	cinnamon, to taste
	raspberry or strawberry syrup, warmed

Lay bread slices on a flat surface. Spread 4 pieces with about I tablespoon cream cheese spread. Press raspberries into cream cheese or spread I tablespoon jam over top. Cover with remaining bread slices and press together.

In a pie pan, whisk together the eggs, milk, and cinnamon. Dip each side of the stuffed French toast in the egg mixture and then cook in a large skillet until golden brown on both sides. When done, serve on individual plates with syrup drizzled over top. Makes 4 servings.

*Blueberries or sliced strawberries may be substituted, as well as other jams.

GRANDPA'S EGGS ALA GOLDENROD

12	**eggs**
4 tablespoons	**margarine or butter**
4 tablespoons	**flour**
$1/2$ teaspoon	**dry mustard**
$1/2$ teaspoon	**salt**
$1/4$ teaspoon	**white pepper**
2 cups	**milk**
2 cups	**grated cheddar cheese (or your favorite cheese),** plus more for garnish
6	**English muffins,** split

Hard boil the eggs and keep warm. Place margarine in a medium saucepan and melt over medium-low heat. Blend in flour, dry mustard, salt, and pepper. Stir until well blended.

Add the milk, a little at a time, stirring constantly until mixture is smooth, bubbly, and thickened. Add cheese and stir until melted.

Toast the English muffins and then top each muffin half with 1 chopped hard-boiled egg, cheese sauce, and extra cheese. Makes 6 servings.

PUMPKIN CREAM CHEESE MUFFINS

I package (8 ounces)	**cream cheese,** room temperature
I cup	**powdered sugar**
2 $\frac{1}{4}$ cups	**flour**
2 cups	**sugar**
$\frac{1}{2}$ teaspoon	**salt**
2 teaspoons	**baking powder**
$\frac{1}{4}$ teaspoon	**baking soda**
I tablespoon	**pumpkin pie spice**
2	**eggs**
I can (15 ounces)	**pumpkin**
$\frac{3}{4}$ cup	**oil**
$\frac{1}{2}$ teaspoon	**vanilla**

In a bowl, beat together the cream cheese and powdered sugar until smooth; set aside. In a second bowl, mix together the flour, sugar, salt, baking powder, baking soda, and pie spice. In a third bowl, whisk together the eggs, pumpkin, oil, and vanilla. Stir into dry ingredients until smooth.

Fill muffin tins about one-third full of batter and then drop a teaspoon of cream cheese filling in the center. Top off with a little more batter so muffin cup is two-thirds full. Bake at 350 degrees 20–25 minutes, or until a toothpick inserted in the center comes out clean. Makes about 24 muffins.

VARIATION: Add a streusel topping! Just combine $\frac{1}{2}$ cup sugar, $\frac{1}{4}$ cup flour, 4 tablespoons cold butter, and I $\frac{1}{2}$ teaspoons cinnamon. Mix with a fork until crumbly. Sprinkle over muffins before baking.

EGG WHITE OMELETS

8	**egg whites**
2–3 tablespoons	**milk**
1/4 cup	**cottage cheese**
	salt and pepper, to taste
1/2 cup	**toppings, such as cooked bacon or sausage, or diced ham, peppers, onions, mushrooms, grated cheese, etc.**

Mix together the egg whites, milk, and cottage cheese. Season with salt and pepper. Pour half of the egg mixture into a heated saucepan sprayed generously with nonstick spray and let cook, swirling the pan occasionally to move uncooked egg to outer edge. Just before the egg is almost cooked and starting to brown slightly underneath, top half of it with desired toppings and then fold the remaining half of cooked egg over top. Let cook a couple minutes longer and then serve. Makes 2 omelets.

QUICHE

½	**large onion,** roughly chopped
4–5	**mushrooms,** thinly sliced
1 tablespoon	**olive oil**
½ teaspoon	**minced garlic**
1 (9-inch)	**premade piecrust**
1½ cups	**grated Swiss cheese**
4	**eggs**
1½ cups	**half-and-half**
	salt and pepper, to taste

Preheat oven to 425 degrees.

Saute the onion and mushrooms in oil until caramelized, about 3–5 minutes. Stir in garlic and then put mixture in the bottom of the piecrust. Cover with the cheese.

Beat eggs and half-and-half together with salt and pepper. Pour egg mixture over the cheese.

Bake 15 minutes, reduce the oven temperature to 300 degrees, and then bake 30–35 minutes longer, or until center is set. Let stand a few minutes before serving. Makes 6–8 servings.

VARIATION: Add cooked diced ham or bacon.

FRUIT AND CREAMY DIP

1 package (8 ounces)	**cream cheese,** room temperature
1 container (6 ounces)	**lemon yogurt**
1 jar (7 ounces)	**marshmallow crème**
¼ cup	**pineapple juice**
1 cup	**whipped topping**
	strawberries, apples, pineapple, grapes, bananas, etc.

In a bowl, blend together the cream cheese, yogurt, marshmallow crème, and pineapple juice. Gently fold in the whipped topping.

Chill 1–2 hours and then serve with fruit. Makes 8–10 servings.

CHEESE BLINTZES

2	**eggs**
2 tablespoons	**oil**
1 cup	**milk**
3/4 cup	**flour**
1/2 teaspoon	**salt**
1 tablespoon	**sugar**
4 ounces	**cream cheese,** softened
1 cup	**ricotta cheese**
1/4 cup	**sugar**
1 teaspoon	**vanilla**
	sour cream, berries, jam, powdered sugar, etc.

Beat together the eggs, oil, and milk. Add flour, salt, and sugar; beat until smooth. Chill batter for 30 minutes.

Spray a crepe pan or an 8-inch skillet with nonstick spray. Pour just under 1/3 cup batter onto pan and swirl to completely coat pan. Flip once crepe has lightly browned and cook until second side is done. Repeat until all batter is used.

Preheat oven to 350 degrees.

Beat together the cream cheese, ricotta cheese, sugar, and vanilla until smooth. Fill each crepe evenly with filling. Fold in the ends and then roll like a burrito. Place filled crepes in a 9 x 13-inch pan prepared with nonstick spray.

Bake 15–20 minutes, or until warmed through. Garnish individual servings with sour cream, berries, jam, powdered sugar, or whatever is desired. Makes 4–6 servings.

BACON, EGG, AND CHEESE BISCUITS

1 tube (16 ounces)	**refrigerated large buttermilk biscuits**
6	**eggs**
	butter or margarine, optional
6 slices	**American cheese**
6 slices	**cooked bacon**

Bake biscuits according to package directions.

While biscuits bake, fry the eggs. When biscuits are done, cut in half and butter, if desired. Place a cheese slice on the bottom half of biscuit, top with a warm egg, add a piece of bacon, and top with other half of biscuit. Serve warm. Makes 6 sandwiches.

MINI PANCAKE STACKS

2 cups	**pancake mix**
I cup	**milk**
2	**eggs**
I container (8 ounces)	**cheesecake-flavored cream cheese spread**
	boysenberry syrup, warm

In a bowl, combine pancake mix, milk, and eggs.

Heat a large skillet and spray with nonstick spray. Cook 3-inch round pancakes using all the batter; keep warm.

Place a warm pancake in the center of each plate and top with a thick layer of cream cheese spread. Repeat two more times so you have 3 pancakes stacked on each plate and cream cheese spread on top of each. Pour warm syrup over top and serve. Makes 4–6 servings.

VARIATION: Use any syrup your family likes—they all taste delicious!

BREAKFAST CASSEROLE

1 package (32 ounces)	**shredded hash browns,** cooked according to package directions
1/2 pound	**sausage,** browned and drained
1/2 pound	**bacon,** cooked and crumbled
10–12	**eggs**
	salt and pepper, to taste
1 1/2–2 cups	**grated cheddar cheese**

Preheat oven to 350 degrees.

Place prepared hash browns in the bottom of a 9 x 13-inch pan prepared with nonstick spray. Spread the sausage and bacon over top.

Scramble the eggs in a skillet until almost cooked through. Season with salt and pepper and then stir in 1/2 cup cheese. Pour eggs over meats and spread remaining cheese over top to cover. Bake 30 minutes. Serve with ketchup, if desired. Makes 8–10 servings.

VARIATIONS: You can use 1 pound of any favorite breakfast meat such as sausage, bacon, or ham, or any combination of breakfast meats to equal 1 pound.

APPETIZERS

TERRY'S TOTALLY YUMMY CHEESEBALL

2 packages (8 ounces each)	**cream cheese,** room temperature
4 tablespoons	**butter or margarine,** room temperature
2 cups	**finely grated cheddar cheese**
2 tablespoons	**milk**
2 tablespoons	**finely chopped green onions**
2 tablespoons	**chopped pimientos**
2 teaspoons	**Worcestershire sauce**
I dash	**hot pepper sauce**
I cup	**chopped walnuts or pecans**

Mix together the cream cheese and butter. Stir in all the remaining ingredients except the nuts and mix well. Cover and chill 4–24 hours.

Shape into a ball and roll in nuts. Serve with your favorite crackers. Makes 12–15 servings.

JALAPEÑO POPPERS

1 package (8 ounces)	**cream cheese,** room temperature
1 cup	**grated pepper jack cheese**
16	**jalapeño peppers,** seeded and halved
1/2 cup or more	**milk**
1/2 cup or more	**flour**
1/2 cup or more	**breadcrumbs**
	oil, for frying

In a medium bowl, mix together the cheeses. Spoon this mixture into the halved jalapeños.

Put the milk and flour and breadcrumbs into separate bowls. Dip the stuffed jalapeños first into the milk then into the flour, making sure they are well coated with each. Set on paper towels to let dry for about 10 minutes.

Dip stuffed jalapeños a second time in milk and then roll in the breadcrumbs; let dry. Dip a third time in milk and then roll in breadcrumbs again until completely coated with breadcrumbs.

In a medium skillet, heat the oil until it is hot but not smoking. Deep-fry the coated jalapeños 2–3 minutes each, or until golden brown. Remove and let drain on paper towels. Serve hot. Makes 16 servings.

MOZZARELLA STICKS

2	**eggs**
1 1/2 cups	**Italian seasoned breadcrumbs**
1/2 teaspoon	**garlic powder**
8 sticks	**mozzarella string cheese,** cut in half
	oil, for deep-frying

In a small bowl, beat the eggs and set aside. In a separate bowl, mix the breadcrumbs and garlic powder.

In a heavy saucepan, heat oil until it is hot but not smoking. Dip each mozzarella stick in the egg and then in the breadcrumbs. Let dry and then repeat so the cheese sticks are double coated.

Heat oil in a deep-fryer until hot. Fry coated cheese in batches until golden brown, about 30–45 seconds. Remove from heat and drain on paper towels. Serve hot with warm marinara sauce for dipping, if desired. Makes 8 servings.

CHEESY FONDUE

2 cups	**shredded Gruyere cheese**
2 cups	**shredded Swiss cheese**
3 tablespoons	**flour**
1/2 teaspoon	**dry mustard**
3/4 cup	**sparkling apple cider**
1/2 teaspoon	**Worcestershire sauce**

Mix all ingredients in a fondue pot. Heat until cheese is melted and fondue is warmed through. Add more cider if fondue is too thick, or add a little more flour if fondue is too thin. Serve with raw vegetables or chunks of bread for dipping. Makes 8 servings.

BLUE CHEESE AND BACON DIP

6–7 slices	**bacon**
2 cloves	**garlic,** minced
1 package (8 ounces)	**cream cheese,** softened
¼ cup	**half-and-half**
1 cup	**blue cheese crumbles**
2 tablespoons	**chopped fresh chives**

Cook bacon in a large skillet over medium-high heat until crisp. Drain on paper towels. When cool enough to handle, crumble bacon. Drain excess fat from skillet and add garlic. Cook garlic about 3 minutes.

Preheat oven to 350 degrees. In a medium-size bowl, beat cream cheese until smooth. Add half-and-half and mix until combined. Stir in crumbled bacon, garlic, blue cheese, and chives. Transfer to a small ovenproof serving dish and cover with foil.

Bake until thoroughly heated, about 30 minutes. Serve with crackers, French bread, or apple slices. Makes 6–8 servings.

BAKED BRIE

I package	**frozen puff pastry sheets,** room temperature
I	**egg**
I tablespoon	**water**
I wheel (15 ounces)	**Brie**
	egg wash (egg mixed with a small amount of water or milk)

Preheat oven to 350 degrees.

Whisk together egg and water in a small bowl. Open and flatten pastry sheets. Place wheel of Brie in the center and wrap pastry sheets to cover it. Cut off excess pastry dough and form loose ends of dough together to make a seam. Seal seam with egg wash.

Place wrapped Brie seam side down on a baking sheet. Brush top and sides with egg wash and bake 20 minutes, or until pastry is golden brown. Let stand I hour before serving. Serve with red grapes or a little raspberry jam on the side. Makes 8 servings.

MINI CHEDDAR BISCUITS

2 cups	**biscuit baking mix**
1 cup	**shredded cheddar cheese**
1/2 teaspoon	**garlic powder**
2/3 cup	**milk**
2 tablespoons	**butter or margarine,** melted
1 teaspoon	**garlic salt**

Preheat oven to 400 degrees. Spray a baking sheet with nonstick cooking spray and set aside.

In a large bowl, combine baking mix, cheese, and garlic powder. Stir in milk. Roll out dough on a floured surface. Cut biscuits with 1-inch round cookie cutters into desired shapes. Place on prepared baking sheet.

Bake 10 minutes. Remove and brush biscuits with melted butter. Sprinkle with garlic salt. Bake 5 minutes more, or until lightly browned. Makes 12 biscuits.

MINI QUICHES

1 box	**refrigerated piecrust**
1 cup	**cubed ham**
¼ cup	**chopped green onions**
3	**eggs**
	salt and pepper, to taste
1 cup	**half-and-half**
1 cup	**grated cheddar cheese**

Cut piecrust in 24 small circles to fit into the bottoms of mini muffin cups.

Cook bacon until crispy. Drain on paper towels. Drain all but 2 table-spoons bacon grease from pan. When bacon is cool enough to handle, crumble into pieces and return to frying pan. Add mushrooms and onions, and saute over medium heat for just a few minutes. Spoon a little into each muffin cup.

In a bowl, beat eggs, salt, and pepper; add half-and-half and mix well. Fill each mini muffin cup with the mixture until almost full. Sprinkle cheese over top. Bake at 375 degrees 20–30 minutes, or until done. Makes 8 servings.

CAPRESE BITES

I basket	**cherry tomatoes**
I container (I2 ounces)	**mini fresh mozzarella balls**
	fresh basil leaves
	extra virgin olive oil
	balsamic vinegar
	salt and pepper, to taste

On toothpicks or appetizer toothpicks, spear I tomato, I mini mozzarella ball, and I basil leaf. Repeat until all the tomatoes and/or cheese are used. Set on serving tray. Drizzle with oil and vinegar, and sprinkle with salt and pepper. Makes 16 servings.

SPICY QUESO

1	**onion,** diced
2 tablespoons	**oil**
1 can (10 ounces)	**diced Rotel tomatoes**
1 can (4 ounces)	**diced green chiles**
1	**clove garlic,** minced
1 pound	**processed American cheese,** cubed

Saute onion in oil until transparent. Stir in the tomatoes and chiles, and simmer 15–20 minutes. Add the garlic and saute a few minutes more. Stir in cheese until melted. Serve with chips. Makes 16–20 servings.

SPENCE'S CHEESY CHIP DIP

I can (15 ounces)	**refried beans**
I can (15 ounces)	**black beans,** rinsed and drained
I can (10 ounces)	**diced Rotel tomatoes,** drained
I can (4 ounces)	**green chiles**
I can (3.8 ounces)	**sliced or diced olives**
I cup	**grated Monterey Jack cheese**
I cup	**grated cheddar cheese**
	shredded lettuce, optional
	sour cream, optional
	diced avocado, optional

Spread the refried beans in the bottom of a deep glass dish. Sprinkle black beans over top. Layer tomatoes, green chiles, and olives over top. Then layer with the cheeses.

Place container in the microwave and heat about 3–5 minutes until cheese has melted. Once cheese is melted and the dip is completely warmed through, it is ready to serve. Garnish with lettuce, sour cream, and avocado, if desired. Serve with tortilla chips for dipping. Makes 8 servings.

STUFFED MUSHROOMS

I pound	**spicy Italian sausage**
1/3 cup	**Italian breadcrumbs**
1/4 cup	**grated Parmesan cheese,** plus more
1/4 cup	**grated mozzarella cheese**
I teaspoon	**minced garlic**
30	**mushrooms,** stems removed
2 teaspoons	**olive oil**

Preheat the oven to 350 degrees.

In a frying pan, cook the sausage until crumbly and brown. Place cooked sausage in a bowl and then stir in the breadcrumbs and cheeses until well combined.

Saute the garlic and mushrooms in olive oil for just a few minutes so they are slightly cooked. Place mushrooms on a baking sheet and fill with the sausage stuffing. Sprinkle extra Parmesan cheese over top and then bake 15 minutes. Makes 10 servings.

SPINACH AND ARTICHOKE DIP

1 jar (14 ounces)	**artichoke hearts,** drained and chopped
1/2 package (10 ounces)	**frozen chopped spinach,** thawed and drained
1/2 cup	**sour cream**
1/4 cup	**mayonnaise**
4 ounces	**cream cheese**
1/2 cup	**grated Romano cheese**
1/2 teaspoon	**minced garlic**
	salt and pepper, to taste

Preheat the oven to 375 degrees. Lightly coat a baking dish with non-stick cooking spray.

In a bowl, mix together all ingredients and then pour into prepared baking dish. Bake 20–25 minutes, or until heated through and lightly browned on top. Makes 12–14 servings.

CREAMY FRUIT DIP

1 package (8 ounces)	**cream cheese,** softened
3 tablespoons	**sugar**
1 cup	**sour cream or mascarpone cheese**
1 teaspoon	**vanilla or almond extract**

Combine all ingredients and beat until smooth and creamy. Serve with fresh fruit for dipping. Makes 12 servings.

LISA'S GOAT CHEESE AND OLIVE TAPENADE

1 jar (3 ounces)	**green olives with pimientos**
1/2 can (6 ounces)	**black olives**
1–2 cloves	**garlic**
1/4 cup	**red wine vinegar**
squeeze	**lemon juice**
	black pepper, to taste
2 teaspoons	**olive oil**
8 ounces	**goat cheese**

To make tapenade, put everything but the goat cheese into a food processor and chop. Serve with goat cheese and sliced bread or crostini slices. Makes 6–8 servings.

SOUPS

WISCONSIN CHEESE SOUP

2 cups	**sliced carrots**
2 cups	**chopped broccoli**
2 cups	**chicken broth**
1/2 cup	**chopped onion**
1/4 cup plus 2 tablespoons	**butter**
1/4 cup plus 2 tablespoons	**flour**
1/4 teaspoon	**ground black pepper**
3 cups	**milk**
1 pound	**Velveeta cheese,** cubed
1/8–1/4 teaspoon	**cayenne pepper**
1/2 teaspoon	**dry mustard**

In a small saucepan over medium-high heat, combine carrots, broccoli, and chicken broth. Bring to a boil. Cover, reduce heat, and simmer 5 minutes. Remove from heat and set aside.

In a large saucepan, cook onion in butter over medium heat until onion is translucent. Stir in flour and pepper. Add milk and stir continuously over medium heat until soup is thickened. Stir in cheese, cayenne pepper, and mustard, and heat through. Makes 4–6 servings.

WHITE CHEDDAR BROCCOLI SOUP

2–3 teaspoons	**olive oil**
1/3 cup	**chopped onion**
I teaspoon	**minced garlic**
5 cups	**broccoli florets**
4 cups	**chicken broth**
3/4 cup	**water**
2 cups	**half-and-half**
2 1/2 cups	**grated white cheddar cheese**
1/2 cup	**flour**
1/4 teaspoon	**ground black pepper**
	salt, to taste

In a frying pan, heat the oil and saute onion and garlic until tender. Add broccoli and saute a few minutes more, making sure the broccoli is still crisp.

In a large pot over medium-high heat, combine the broth, water, half-and-half, cheese, flour, and pepper. Whisk together to break up any lumps. Bring to a boil and reduce heat to low. Stir in the broccoli mixture and simmer 15 minutes, or until broccoli is tender. Add salt to taste. Makes 4–6 servings.

CHEESY CHICKEN CORN CHOWDER

1/4 cup plus 2 tablespoons	**butter**
1/2 cup	**diced onion**
1/4 cup plus 2 tablespoons	**flour**
4 1/2 cups	**milk**
2 cups	**shredded rotisserie chicken**
1 can (15 ounces)	**Niblets corn,** drained
1 can (4 ounces)	**diced green chiles**
1 1/2 cups	**Monterey Jack cheese**
	salt and pepper, to taste

In a large soup pot, melt butter over medium heat. Saute onion in butter until soft. Stir in flour and cook 2 minutes. Gradually stir in milk. Return to heat and cook, stirring constantly, until thickened. Stir in chicken, corn, chiles, and cheese. Season with salt and pepper. Cook until cheese is melted; ladle into soup bowls and serve. Makes 6 servings.

FRENCH ONION SOUP

³/₄ cup	**butter**
2 tablespoons	**olive oil**
5–6 cups	**thinly sliced onions**
I clove	**garlic,** minced
6 cans (10.5 ounces each)	**beef broth**
I tablespoon	**Worcestershire sauce**
I teaspoon	**thyme,** optional
6 slices	**French bread,** toasted
2–3 cups	**shredded Gruyere cheese**

Melt the butter with olive oil in large soup pan over medium heat. Add onions and stir occasionally until browned and nicely caramelized, about 30 minutes. Add garlic and cook a few minutes more. Add the broth, Worcestershire sauce, and thyme, if using, and simmer 20 minutes more.

Heat the oven to broil. Ladle the soup into oven-safe bowls and float the toasted bread on top. Layer ¹/₂ cup cheese over each slice of bread. Place bowls on a baking sheet and broil until the cheese bubbles and is slightly brown. Makes 6 servings.

SWISS CHEESE AND SAUSAGE SOUP

1 pound	**sausage**
1	**onion,** diced
6	**red potatoes,** unpeeled and cubed
1 cup	**diced leek**
4–5 cans (14 ounces each)	**chicken broth**
1 pound	**Swiss cheese,** grated
1 can (12 ounces)	**evaporated milk**
	salt and pepper, to taste

In a frying pan, brown the sausage and then stir in the onion; saute a few minutes until tender. Scoop mixture into a bowl lined with paper towels and set aside.

Place the potatoes and leek into a soup pot. Pour in enough broth to cover the vegetables by 1 inch. Bring to a boil and simmer over medium heat 15 minutes. Add the sausage and onion mixture, and cook 10–15 minutes more, or until potatoes are tender. Reduce heat to low and stir in cheese and evaporated milk. Cook until just heated through and cheese is melted. Makes 6 servings.

CREAMY CAULIFLOWER SOUP

I can (15 ounces)	**chicken broth** (or 2 1/2 cups water)
2 cups	**chopped cauliflower**
2 cups	**peeled and cubed potatoes**
3/4 cup	**finely chopped celery**
1/2 cup	**chopped onion**
1/4 cup plus 2 tablespoons	**butter**
1/4 cup plus 2 tablespoons	**flour**
4 1/2 cups	**whole milk**
	salt and pepper, to taste
I cup	**grated cheddar cheese**

In a large saucepan, combine the chicken broth or water and vegetables. Cover and bring to a boil. Boil 10–12 minutes, or until vegetables are tender; set aside.

In a large soup pot, melt butter over medium heat. Stir in flour and cook 2 minutes. Remove from heat and gradually stir in milk. Return to heat and cook, stirring constantly, until thickened. Stir in vegetables with cooking liquid; season with salt and pepper. Stir in cheese until melted and remove from heat. Makes 6 servings.

SPINACH AND
BLUE CHEESE SOUP

³/₄ cup	**chopped onion**
2 tablespoons	**olive oil**
¹/₂ cup	**flour**
6 cups	**chicken broth**
2 cups	**milk**
4 ounces	**blue cheese,** crumbled
1 package (10 ounces)	**frozen chopped spinach,** thawed
¹/₂ cup	**heavy cream**
	salt, to taste
¹/₂ teaspoon	**nutmeg**
¹/₂ teaspoon	**cayenne pepper**
6 strips	**bacon,** cooked and crumbled

In a large pot over medium heat, saute onion in olive oil about 3 minutes. Add flour and stir well until mixed. Add broth, raise heat to high, and bring to a boil.

Add milk, reduce heat to medium, and simmer 5 minutes. Add the cheese and stir until blended; then add the spinach and cook 3 minutes more. Add the cream, bring just to a boil, turn off heat, and stir well. Add salt, nutmeg, and cayenne pepper. Ladle into individual bowls and sprinkle with bacon. Makes 4–6 servings.

BAKED POTATO SOUP

¹/₄ cup plus 2 tablespoons	**butter**
¹/₂ cup	**diced onion**
¹/₄ cup	**finely diced carrot**
¹/₄ cup plus 2 tablespoons	**flour**
I quart	**half-and-half**
2	**large potatoes,** baked
4 strips	**bacon,** cooked and crumbled, divided
I ¹/₂ cups	**grated cheddar cheese,** plus more for garnish

Melt butter in a soup pot and add onion and carrot; cook until tender. Stir in flour. Cook 2 minutes more. Add half-and-half; cook, stirring constantly, until thickened. Scoop out centers of baked potatoes and add to soup. Roughly chop skins and add. Stir in half the cooked bacon and I cup cheese. Ladle into soup bowls. Garnish with remaining bacon and cheese. Makes 4 servings.

TOMATO CREAM CHEESE SOUP

1	**medium onion,** chopped
2 tablespoons	**butter or margarine**
1–2 cloves	**garlic,** minced
2 cans (14.5 ounces each)	**crushed tomatoes**
2 cans (14 ounces each)	**Progresso tomato soup**
1/2 tablespoon	**fresh chopped basil or**
	2 teaspoons dried basil
1/2 teaspoon	**paprika**
1 package (8 ounces)	**mascarpone or cream cheese,** cubed

In a saucepan, saute onion in butter until tender. Add garlic and cook a few minutes more. Add remaining ingredients except cheese and heat through. Stir in cheese until melted. Serve immediately. Makes 6–8 servings.

CHICKEN, BROCCOLI, AND WILD RICE SOUP

I cup	**wild rice**
6 cups	**chicken broth**
I package (10 ounces)	**frozen chopped broccoli,** thawed
I–I½ cups	**thinly sliced carrots**
¼ cup	**diced onion**
I can (10.5 ounces)	**cream of chicken soup,** condensed
I package (8 ounces)	**cream cheese,** cut into chunks
I½–2 cups	**rotisserie chicken,** cut into bite-size pieces
	water, if needed

In a large soup pan, combine rice and broth, and bring to a boil. Reduce heat, cover, and simmer 10–15 minutes, stirring occasionally. Stir in the broccoli, carrots, and onion. Cover and simmer 10 minutes, or until vegetables are tender. Stir in the soup, cream cheese, and chicken. Cook and stir until cheese is melted. Thin with water if soup is too thick. Makes 6–8 servings.

THREE-CHEESE POTATO SOUP

6	**potatoes,** peeled and cubed
I cup	**finely chopped carrots**
I cup	**finely chopped celery**
3 cups	**chicken broth or vegetable broth**
	salt, to taste
2 cups	**milk**
3 tablespoons	**butter or margarine,** melted
4 tablespoons	**flour**
2 teaspoons	**Montreal Steak Seasoning**
I teaspoon	**black pepper**
I cup each	**grated cheddar, Monterey Jack, and Gouda cheeses**

In a large pot over medium heat, combine the potatoes, carrots, celery, broth, and salt. Bring to a boil and then reduce heat; cover and simmer until potatoes are tender, about 15–20 minutes. Stir in milk.

In a small bowl, combine butter, flour, steak seasoning, and pepper. Stir into soup over medium heat. Cook, stirring until thick and bubbly. Remove from heat and stir in cheeses until melted. Makes 4–6 servings.

NACHO CHEESE SOUP

1 pound	**ground beef**
1	**red or green bell pepper,** chopped
1	**small yellow onion,** chopped
1 jar (15 ounces)	**Queso dip**
1 can (10.5 ounces)	**nacho cheese soup,** condensed
4 cups	**milk**
1 can (11 ounces)	**Niblets corn**

Cook ground beef, bell pepper, and onion together in a soup pot. Drain fat. Stir in remaining ingredients and heat through. Serve with tortilla chips. Makes 4–6 servings.

SALADS

STRAWBERRY AND BLUE CHEESE SALAD

1 head	**romaine lettuce,** torn into bite-size pieces
1 container (1 pound)	**strawberries,** washed and sliced
3/4–1 cup	**blue cheese crumbles**
1/2–3/4 cup	**sliced honey-roasted almonds**
1 bottle	**poppy seed dressing**

In a large bowl, layer the lettuce, strawberries, cheese, and almonds. Just before serving, toss with the desired amount of dressing. Makes 8–10 servings.

ORZO SALAD WITH FETA

1 cup	**uncooked orzo pasta**
1/2 cup	**sliced green olives**
1 cup	**crumbled feta cheese**
1/4 cup	**chopped fresh parsley**
6–8	**cherry tomatoes,** halved or quartered
1	**yellow bell pepper,** seeded and cut into cubes*
1 cup	**Greek vinaigrette (or other favorite vinaigrette)**

Cook the orzo according to package directions; rinse and drain. When cool, combine the orzo in a bowl with the olives, cheese, parsley, tomatoes, and bell pepper. Toss with the dressing and serve. Makes 4–6 servings.

*Substitute 1/2 cup chopped roasted red pepper, or more if desired.

PEAR, GORGONZOLA, AND CANDIED PECAN SALAD

I head	**romaine or leafy green lettuce,** torn into bite-size pieces
2	**pears,** washed and cut into bite-size pieces*
3/4–I cup	**crumbled Gorgonzola cheese**
I cup	**candied pecans**
3/4 cup	**dried cranberries or cherries**
3/4 cup	**real bacon crumbles**
	red wine vinaigrette

In a large bowl, layer all salad ingredients.

Just before serving, toss with the dressing. Makes 8 servings.

*Toss with a little lemon juice to prevent browning.

COTTAGE CHEESE SALAD

1 container (16 ounces)	**cottage cheese**
	garlic powder, to taste
	salt and pepper, to taste
1/2 teaspoon	**dill,** optional
4	**iceberg lettuce leaves,** left whole
8–10	**cherry tomatoes,** halved or quartered depending on size
1	**cucumber,** sliced or chopped
1/2 cup	**chopped celery**

In a bowl, combine the cottage cheese and seasonings; chill. Scoop 1/2 cup cottage cheese mixture into each lettuce leaf. Top each with tomatoes, cucumber, and celery, and then serve. Makes 4 servings.

VARIATION: Sprinkle cooked and crumbled bacon over top.

BBQ CHICKEN AND SMOKED GOUDA SALAD

½–1 pound	**grilled chicken breast,** cut into cubes
½ cup	**BBQ sauce,** plus more
1 head	**leafy green or romaine lettuce,** torn into pieces
4–8 ounces	**smoked Gouda cheese,** cut into small cubes
1–2	**avocados,** diced*
½	**red onion,** thinly sliced
½ cup	**real bacon bits**
	ranch dressing

Toss the chicken in BBQ sauce. Layer the lettuce, chicken, cheese, avocado, onion, and bacon on individual serving plates. Serve with ranch dressing and more BBQ sauce on the side. Makes 8–10 servings.

*Toss with a little lemon juice to prevent browning.

VARIATION: Add diced tomato or red bell pepper.

SIMPLE GOAT CHEESE SALAD

I bag (6 ounces)	**baby spinach**
2 cups	**halved seedless red grapes**
I container (6 ounces)	**goat cheese,** crumbled
I cup	**coarsely chopped candied pecans***
	raspberry vinaigrette dressing

Layer all salad ingredients except dressing in a large bowl. Toss with dressing just before serving, or allow individuals to dress their own salads. Makes 8–10 servings.

*Walnuts and cashews may be substituted.

SOUTHWEST LAYERED SALAD

1 head	**romaine lettuce,** torn into bite-size pieces
2 cups	**grated pepper jack cheese**
1 can (15 ounces)	**black beans,** rinsed and drained
1 cup	**frozen corn,** thawed
1	**large red bell pepper,** diced
1 cup	**crushed Fritos corn chips**
	ranch dressing
	salsa

In a large bowl, layer the lettuce, cheese, beans, corn, bell pepper, and chips. Combine 2 parts ranch dressing with 1 part salsa (or more if desired). Serve dressing on the side or toss just before serving. Makes 8–10 servings.

VARIATION: For a heartier salad, add a layer of grilled chicken cooked with a little taco seasoning or with lime juice, salt, and pepper.

CHEESY BROCCOLI AND BACON SALAD

Dressing:

1 cup	**mayonnaise**
2 tablespoons	**red wine vinegar**
1/2 cup	**sugar**

Salad:

6 cups	**broccoli florets**
1 1/2 cups	**red grape halves**
1/2	**red onion,** chopped or thinly sliced
1 pound	**bacon,** cooked and crumbled
2 1/2 cups	**grated sharp cheddar cheese**
3/4–1 cup	**cashew pieces**

In a bowl, combine all the dressing ingredients together and set aside.

In a large bowl, combine all the salad ingredients. Pour dressing over top and stir. Refrigerate 1 hour before serving for flavors to blend. Makes 8–10 servings.

GREEK SALAD

1	**cucumber,** halved and then sliced
1 container (6 ounces)	**crumbled feta cheese**
$^1/_2$ cup	**kalamata olives,** pitted
1 cup	**chopped Roma tomatoes**
$^1/_2$	**red onion,** thinly sliced
$^1/_2$ cup	**balsamic vinaigrette or Greek salad dressing**
6 cups	**torn romaine lettuce**

Toss all ingredients together except the lettuce in a large bowl and let chill 1–2 hours before serving. Remove from refrigerator, toss in lettuce, and serve. Add more dressing to coat, if necessary. Makes 6–8 servings.

CAPRESE SALAD

3–4	**large tomatoes,** cut into slices
2 pounds	**fresh mozzarella,** cut into slices
1/4 cup	**freshly chopped basil**
	balsamic vinaigrette
	salt and pepper, to taste

On a platter, alternate the tomato and mozzarella slices. Sprinkle with basil and then drizzle desired amount of balsamic vinaigrette over top. Season with salt and pepper. Makes 6–8 servings.

TORTELLINI PASTA SALAD

Dressing:

³/₄ cup	**sugar**
³/₄ cup	**mayonnaise**
I tablespoon	**cider vinegar**

Salad:

3 cups	**broccoli florets**
³/₄ cup	**diced roasted red peppers**
I pound	**chicken,** cooked and cubed
I package (I3 ounces)	**cheese tortellini,** cooked and cooled
I pound	**bacon,** cooked and crumbled
¹/₂ cup	**sunflower seeds**
I cup	**crumbled feta cheese**

In a small bowl, combine the sugar, mayonnaise, and vinegar until smooth; set aside.

In a large bowl, combine salad ingredients and then pour dressing over top. Chill I–2 hours before serving. Makes 6 servings.

VARIATION: Make extra dressing for an extra creamy salad.

FETA PASTA SALAD

12 ounces	**penne or rotini pasta,** cooked and cooled
1	**green bell pepper,** diced
1	**red bell pepper,** diced
1	**container grape tomatoes***
1 cup	**firmly packed fresh baby spinach**
1 container (6 ounces)	**crumbled feta cheese**
1–1½ cups	**Caesar salad dressing**

Gently combine all ingredients until nicely coated with dressing. Refrigerate until ready to serve; add more dressing to moisten, if necessary. Makes 8 servings.

*Substitute ½–1 cup chopped sun-dried tomatoes.

HAM, SWISS, AND ARTICHOKE PASTA SALAD

1 jar (14.5 ounces)	**marinated artichoke hearts,** quartered
2 cups	**cubed ham**
4–6 ounces	**Swiss cheese,** cubed
$^3/_4$ cup	**minced fresh parsley**
10–12 ounces	**rotini pasta,** cooked and cooled
1$^1/_2$ tablespoons	**Dijon mustard**
$^1/_3$ cup	**olive oil**
	salt and pepper, to taste

Drain the artichoke hearts and reserve about $^1/_2$ cup of the marinade.

In a large bowl, toss together the artichoke hearts, ham, cheese, parsley, and pasta.

Combine reserved marinade, mustard, and olive oil. Toss with salad ingredients and then season with salt and pepper. Chill until ready to serve. Makes 6–8 servings.

THREE-CHEESE
BAKED POTATO SALAD

3–3½ pounds	**red or new potatoes,** cooked and cubed
4	**green onions** (green part only), thinly sliced
I cup	**mayonnaise**
I cup	**sour cream**
I tablespoon	**mustard**
¼ cup	**milk**
I pound	**bacon,** cooked and crumbled
4 ounces	**sharp cheddar cheese,** cubed
4 ounces	**Monterey Jack cheese,** cubed
4 ounces	**Swiss or Gruyere cheese,** cubed
	salt and pepper, to taste

In a large bowl, combine the potatoes and green onions; set aside.

In a small bowl, combine the mayonnaise, sour cream, mustard, and milk. Spoon over potato mixture and gently stir until completely covered. Stir in bacon and cheeses, and season with salt and pepper. Chill until ready to serve. Garnish with more green onions and bacon, if desired. Makes 8–10 servings.

GORGONZOLA POTATO SALAD

2 1/2–3 pounds	**red potatoes,** cut into bite-size pieces
1/3 cup	**olive oil**
3 tablespoons	**red wine vinegar**
1 tablespoon	**Dijon mustard**
1 bunch	**chives or 3–4 green onions,** chopped
1 container (5 ounces)	**crumbled Gorgonzola cheese**
1/2 pound	**bacon,** cooked and crumbled
	salt and pepper, to taste

Boil potato pieces in salted water until tender, about 12–15 minutes; drain and cool completely.

In a large bowl, whisk the oil, vinegar, and mustard together until smooth. Add the cooled potatoes, chives, cheese, and bacon. Toss gently to coat. Season with salt and pepper. Makes 6 servings.

BREADS &
SIDES

CHEESY GARLIC BREAD

1/4 cup	**butter or margarine,** softened
3–4 cloves	**garlic,** finely minced
1/2 teaspoon	**Italian seasoning**
6 tablespoons	**grated fresh Parmesan cheese,** divided
1 loaf	**French bread,** sliced in half lengthwise
6–8 slices	**provolone cheese***

Preheat oven to broil.

In a bowl, combine the butter, garlic, seasoning, and 3 tablespoons Parmesan cheese. Evenly spread mixture on cut sides of bread and then place bread on an ungreased baking sheet covered with foil. Sprinkle with remaining Parmesan cheese and then place provolone slices evenly over top. Broil 2–3 minutes, or until golden brown. Serve warm. Makes 6–8 servings.

*Havarti cheese also works well here.

GOOEY ONION-OLIVE BREAD

1/4 cup	**butter or margarine,** softened
4–5 cloves	**garlic,** finely minced
1 loaf	**French bread,** sliced in half lengthwise
1/2–3/4 cup	**chopped onion**
1 teaspoon	**extra virgin olive oil**
1/2 cup	**diced black or green olives**
5 tablespoons	**grated Parmesan cheese**
2–3 cups	**grated mozzarella or provolone cheese**

Preheat oven to broil.

In a bowl, combine the butter and garlic. Evenly spread mixture on cut sides of bread and then place bread on an ungreased baking sheet covered with foil; set aside.

In a frying pan, saute the onion in oil until lightly browned. Stir in olives and then spread evenly over bread. Sprinkle cheeses over top. Broil 2–3 minutes, or until golden brown. Serve warm. Makes 6–8 servings.

CHEDDAR GARLIC BISCUITS

2 cups	**biscuit mix**
1 1/2 cups	**grated sharp cheddar cheese**
2/3 cup	**milk**
3–4 tablespoons	**butter or margarine,** melted
1/4 teaspoon	**garlic powder**

Preheat oven to 450 degrees.

In a bowl, combine the biscuit mix and cheese. Stir in milk until moist. Drop by large spoonfuls onto a lightly sprayed baking sheet or a baking stone. Bake 9–12 minutes, or until golden brown. Combine the butter and garlic powder, and brush over hot biscuits. Serve warm. Makes 6–9 large biscuits.

ITALIAN BISCUIT BITES

I tube (16 ounces)	**jumbo refrigerator buttermilk biscuits**
$^1/_2$ cup	**grated Parmesan cheese**
I teaspoon	**garlic powder**
$^1/_2$ teaspoon	**basil or oregano**
5–6 tablespoons	**butter,** melted
	marinara sauce, for dipping

Preheat oven to 400 degrees.

Cut each biscuit into fourths; set aside. Combine cheese and seasonings, and set aside. Dip each biscuit in butter and then roll in cheese mixture. Bake on a lightly greased baking sheet 10–12 minutes, or until golden brown. Serve warm with marinara sauce on the side. Makes 6–8 servings.

DILL AND CHEDDAR SCONES

2 1/4 cups	**flour**
1 1/2 teaspoons	**baking powder**
1 1/2 teaspoons	**garlic salt**
1/2 cup	**cold butter or margarine,** cubed
3/4 cup	**milk**
2 cups	**grated sharp cheddar cheese**
2 teaspoons	**dill**
	melted butter, optional

Preheat oven to 400 degrees.

In a bowl, combine the flour, baking powder, and garlic salt. Cut in butter until mixture is crumbly.

In another bowl, combine the milk, cheese, and dill. Stir into flour mixture until doughy but still a little crumbly.

Press dough into 6 baseball-size balls and then flatten into triangles that are about 1 inch thick on a greased baking sheet. Bake 18–23 minutes or until golden brown. Brush with melted butter before serving, if desired. Makes 6–8 servings.

PARMESAN GARLIC BREADSTICKS

1 cup	**freshly grated Parmesan cheese**
1 1/2 teaspoons	**garlic salt**
12	**Rhodes freezer rolls,** thawed but still cold
1/2 cup	**butter or margarine,** melted

Combine cheese and garlic salt in a medium bowl; set aside. Roll out each thawed ball of dough into 2-inch-wide strips about 6 inches long. Dip in melted butter and then roll in cheese mixture to coat.

Place in the bottom of a 9 x 13-inch pan. Let rise until about double in size and then cover with any remaining cheese, butter, and more garlic salt, if desired.

Preheat oven to 350 degrees. Bake breadsticks 18–20 minutes, or until lightly browned. Makes 12 servings.

SPICY CORNBREAD

1 box (8.5 ounces)	**cornbread mix**
2 ounces	**canned diced jalapeños**
1 cup	**grated pepper jack cheese**

Make the cornbread batter according to package directions. Stir in the jalapeños and cheese. Pour batter into a greased 8-inch square baking pan. Bake according to package directions, or until a toothpick inserted in the center comes out clean. Cut into squares and serve. Makes 6–9 servings.

ASIAGO MASHED POTATOES

2½ pounds	**russet potatoes,** peeled and boiled
1 tablespoon	**butter**
¼ cup	**milk**
	garlic salt and pepper, to taste
1 teaspoon	**Italian seasoning**
2–3 tablespoons	**sour cream**
¾ cup	**grated Asiago cheese**

Using a potato masher, mash the warm potatoes with the butter and milk. Season with garlic salt, pepper, and Italian seasoning. When creamy, stir in the sour cream and cheese until thoroughly mixed in. Serve warm. Makes 4–6 servings.

EASY CHEESY SPINACH RISOTTO

1–2 tablespoons	**extra virgin olive oil**
2 cloves	**garlic,** minced
1/2	**small yellow onion,** finely chopped
2 cans (14 ounces each)	**chicken broth**
2 cups	**uncooked orzo**
3/4 cup	**grated Romano or Parmesan cheese**
3/4 cup	**grated Colby Jack cheese**
2 cups	**packed chopped spinach**
	salt and pepper, to taste

Heat olive oil in a large saucepan over medium heat. Saute the garlic and onion in oil until tender. Stir broth into the pan and bring to a boil. Add orzo and reduce heat to low. Cover with lid, stirring occasionally, 10–15 minutes, or until orzo has absorbed all the liquid. Add more liquid if mixture seems a little dry. Stir in cheese and spinach, and season with salt and pepper. Serve warm. Makes 6–8 servings.

BAKED CAULIFLOWER

I head	**cauliflower,** cut into florets
2–3 tablespoons	**butter,** cut into pieces
$^1/_4$ cup	**mayonnaise**
I $^1/_2$ tablespoons	**mustard**
$^3/_4$ cup	**grated Parmesan cheese**
I teaspoon	**minced garlic**
$^1/_4$ cup	**grated white cheddar or sharp cheddar cheese**

Preheat oven to 375 degrees.

Steam cauliflower 10–15 minutes, or until slightly tender; drain.

Combine the remaining ingredients except the cheddar cheese and then gently stir in cauliflower. Pour into a 9-inch square pan and sprinkle cheddar over top. Bake about 25 minutes, or until cheese is lightly browned. Makes 4–6 servings.

LAYERED POTATO CASSEROLE

½ cup	**butter,** melted
3–4	**russet potatoes,** peeled and thinly sliced
	garlic salt
	freshly grated Parmesan cheese
2–3	**yams or sweet potatoes,** peeled and thinly sliced

Preheat oven to 425 degrees.

Lightly coat the bottom of a 9 x 13-inch pan with a little melted butter. Cover the bottom of the pan with a layer of russet potatoes. Sprinkle with a little garlic salt and a layer of cheese. Layer some yams or sweet potatoes over top and sprinkle with garlic salt and another layer of cheese. Repeat layers until potatoes are gone and pan is full. Drizzle remaining butter over top. Bake 35–40 minutes, or until potatoes are tender. Makes 10–12 servings.

CREAMY AND CHEESY PAN POTATOES

1 container (16 ounces)	**sour cream**
¼ cup	**butter,** melted
1 teaspoon	**onion powder**
2 cans (10.5 ounces each)	**cream of chicken soup,** condensed
3 cups	**grated cheddar cheese,** divided
1 bag (30 ounces)	**frozen shredded hash browns,** thawed

Preheat oven to 350 degrees. Spray a 9 x 13-inch glass pan with non-stick spray and set aside.

In a large bowl, combine the sour cream, butter, onion powder, and soup. Stir in 2 cups cheese and the hash browns. Pour mixture into prepared pan and spread evenly. Top with remaining cheese and bake, uncovered, 45–50 minutes, or until bubbly around the edges. Makes 10–12 servings.

THREE-CHEESE MASHED POTATOES

2 1/2 pounds	**Yukon gold potatoes,** peeled and boiled
I tablespoon	**butter**
1/4 cup	**milk**
	garlic salt and pepper, to taste
2–3 tablespoons	**sour cream**
1/2 cup	**grated cheddar cheese**
1/4 cup	**grated Asiago cheese**
1/4 cup	**crumbled Gorgonzola cheese**

Using a potato masher, mash the warm potatoes with the butter and milk. Season with garlic salt and pepper. When creamy, stir in the sour cream and cheeses until thoroughly mixed in. Serve warm. Makes 4–6 servings.

PIZZA & PASTAS

CHICKEN PESTO PIZZA

1	**boneless, skinless chicken breast,** cubed and then cooked
2–3 tablespoons	**pesto**
1/4–1/3 cup	**ranch dressing,** divided
1	**Boboli pizza crust**
1 1/2–2 cups	**grated fontina cheese**
	grated Parmesan cheese
	Italian seasoning

Preheat oven to 450 degrees.

Toss together the chicken, pesto, and 1 tablespoon ranch dressing until chicken is coated. Spread remaining ranch dressing evenly onto the Boboli crust; top with the chicken mixture. Sprinkle the fontina and some Parmesan cheese over top. Sprinkle the Italian seasoning over the cheeses. Bake 8–10 minutes, or until cheese is melted. Makes 4 servings.

BBQ CHICKEN PIZZA

1	**boneless, skinless chicken breast,** cubed and then cooked
1/2 cup	**BBQ sauce,** plus more if desired
1	**Boboli pizza crust**
1/3–1/2 cup	**chopped red onion**
1 1/4 cups	**grated mozzarella cheese**
3/4 cup	**grated cheddar, smoked Gouda, or Gouda cheese**

Preheat oven to 450 degrees.

Toss chicken and BBQ sauce together until chicken is coated. Spread a little extra BBQ sauce over the Boboli crust, if desired, and then spread coated chicken evenly over top. Sprinkle with onion and then the cheeses. Bake 8–10 minutes, or until cheese is melted. Makes 4 servings.

GOAT CHEESE AND SUN-DRIED TOMATO PIZZA

1/2 cup	**marinara sauce**
1	**Boboli pizza crust**
1 1/2 cups	**grated mozzarella cheese**
4 ounces	**goat cheese,** crumbled
	sun-dried tomatoes
1/2 cup	**caramelized onions**

Preheat oven to 450 degrees.

Spread the marinara sauce over the Boboli crust. Sprinkle mozzarella over top. Top with the goat cheese, tomatoes, and onions. Bake 8–10 minutes, or until cheese is melted. Makes 4 servings.

CHICKEN CAESAR SALAD PIZZA

1	**refrigerator pizza crust**
3	**chicken breasts,** cooked
1/2 cup	**grated Parmesan cheese,** divided
1/2–3/4 cup	**Caesar salad dressing**
1 teaspoon	**lemon pepper**
1/2 clove	**garlic,** minced
1 package (8 ounces)	**cream cheese,** softened
4 cups	**thinly sliced romaine lettuce**
1 can (4 ounces)	**sliced black olives,** drained

Fit pizza crust on a baking sheet and bake according to package directions.

Slice the chicken into strips; set aside.

In a small bowl, combine 1/4 cup Parmesan cheese, salad dressing, lemon pepper, and garlic.

In a separate bowl, mix together cream cheese and half of dressing mixture. Toss together remaining dressing mixture, lettuce, and olives.

Spread cream cheese mixture over baked crust. Sprinkle lettuce mixture over top. Arrange the sliced chicken pieces over lettuce and then sprinkle with remaining Parmesan cheese. Makes 10–12 servings.

MEXICAN PIZZA

I can (15 ounces)	**refried beans**
1/2–3/4 cup	**chunky salsa**
I	**Boboli pizza crust**
1/2 pound	**hamburger,** browned and drained
2–3 tablespoons	**taco seasoning,** or to taste
1–2 tablespoons	**water**
1/2 can (14.5 ounces)	**diced tomatoes,** drained
1/2 can (4 ounces)	**diced green chiles**
1 1/2 cups	**grated Mexican-blend cheese**
	shredded lettuce, salsa, and sour cream

Preheat oven to 450 degrees.

In a saucepan, warm the beans and salsa together. When mixture has a good consistency, spread half of the bean mixture over the pizza crust and reserve the rest for another use.

In a frying pan, season the hamburger with the taco seasoning and a tablespoon or 2 of water (or according to instructions). Sprinkle meat over beans on crust. Sprinkle tomatoes over meat along with the green chiles. Top with the cheese.

Bake 8–10 minutes, or until cheese is melted. Top individual slices with lettuce, salsa, and sour cream. Makes 4 servings.

NOTE: To use all of the ingredients, make 2 pizzas by doubling the meat and using 2 crusts instead of 1.

ARTICHOKE PIZZA

1	**refrigerator pizza crust**
2–3 tablespoons	**pesto**
8 ounces	**provolone cheese,** grated
1/2 cup	**grated Parmesan cheese**
4	**Roma tomatoes,** sliced
1 can (14.5 ounces)	**artichoke hearts,** drained and chopped
1/4 cup	**fresh basil leaves,** torn
	freshly ground pepper, to taste

Fit pizza crust on a baking sheet and bake according to directions. Brush baked crust with pesto and then layer the cheeses, tomatoes, and artichoke hearts over top. Sprinkle with basil and pepper. Bake 10 minutes, or until cheese is melted and bubbly. Makes 10–12 servings.

GOOD OL' MAC & CHEESE

10–12 ounces	**elbow macaroni**
2 tablespoons	**butter**
2 tablespoons	**flour**
1 cup	**half-and-half or milk**
1 jar (5 ounces)	**Old English cheese**
1 cup	**grated cheddar cheese**
	salt and pepper, to taste

Cook pasta according to package directions and drain; set aside.

Melt the butter in a saucepan over medium heat. Stir in the flour. Pour in the milk, stirring constantly as it thickens. When starting to thicken, gradually stir in Old English cheese until completely melted. Gradually add more half-and-half or milk if sauce is too thick. Stir in cheddar cheese and cooked noodles. Season to taste with salt and pepper. Makes 4–6 servings.

CORDON BLEU BAKE

³/₄–1 pound	**cooked chicken,** cubed
1 cup	**diced ham**
8–10 ounces	**penne pasta,** cooked and drained
2 cups	**heavy cream**
¹/₄ cup	**grated Parmesan cheese**
8 ounces	**Swiss cheese,** grated
	oregano, thyme, and garlic salt, to taste

Preheat oven to 425 degrees.

Put the cooked chicken and ham in a large bowl with the cooked pasta; set aside.

In a saucepan, lightly boil the cream, stirring constantly, for 10 minutes, or until it slightly starts to thicken. Add the Parmesan cheese and half of the Swiss cheese. Stir until cheese is completely melted.

Pour cream sauce over the meats and pasta, and add seasonings. Stir together and pour into a 2-quart casserole. Sprinkle remaining Swiss cheese over top. Bake 10–15 minutes, or until cheese is lightly browned or bubbling on top. Makes 6 servings.

CHICKEN FETTUCINE

12–16 ounces	**fettucine or angel hair pasta**
3 tablespoons	**butter,** melted
½–1 envelope	**Italian dressing mix** (add gradually to taste)
1 cup	**chicken broth**
1 tablespoon	**flour**
1 package (8 ounces)	**cream cheese,** cut into cubes
⅓ cup	**grated fresh Parmesan cheese**
1–1½ pounds	**boneless,** skinless chicken breast, cooked and cubed
1 cup	**peas***

Cook pasta according to package directions; drain and set aside.

In a saucepan, combine butter, dressing mix, broth, and flour. Stir in cream cheese until melted. Add Parmesan cheese and stir until combined. Add chicken and peas, and simmer a few minutes, stirring occasionally. Serve over warm pasta. Makes 4–6 servings.

*Or substitute 1–2 cups steamed broccoli if desired.

PESTO SHRIMP PASTA

I package (8 ounces)	**spaghetti,** broken in half
I cup	**cream or half-and-half**
4–5 tablespoons	**pesto**
¼ cup	**grated Parmesan cheese,** plus more for garnish
I	**onion,** thinly sliced
I tablespoon	**extra virgin olive oil**
1–2 cups	**steamed broccoli**
¾ cup	**grated fontina cheese**
20–30	**shrimp,** cooked with tail shells removed

Cook pasta according to package directions; drain and set aside.

In a saucepan, heat half-and-half for 10 minutes, stirring frequently. Once it is bubbling around the edges, stir in pesto and Parmesan cheese.

In a large skillet, saute the onion in oil until tender. Add the broccoli, cooked spaghetti, pesto sauce, fontina cheese, and shrimp. Stir until heated through and serve. Makes 4–6 servings.

VARIATION: Try substituting asparagus for the broccoli and chicken for the shrimp.

SWISS STROGANOFF

1 bag (12 ounces)	**uncooked egg noodles**
1 pound	**ground beef**
1 tablespoon	**minced onion**
1 can (10.5 ounces)	**cream of mushroom soup,** condensed
1/2 cup	**water**
1 cup	**sour cream**
	paprika, to taste
1 cup	**peas**
1 1/4 cups	**grated Swiss cheese**
	salt and pepper, to taste

Cook noodles according to package directions; drain.

In the meantime, brown the beef with the onion in a frying pan. Drain if necessary. Stir in the soup and water. Once combined, add the sour cream, paprika, peas, cheese, salt, and pepper. Stir until completely heated through and cheese is melted. Serve over hot cooked wide egg noodles. Makes 4–6 servings.

GOOEY LASAGNA

¹/₂	**red bell pepper,** chopped
I jar (I pound, 10 ounces)	**spaghetti sauce**
¹/₂–I pound	**ground Italian sausage,** browned and drained
I package (8 ounces)	**cream cheese,** softened
I cup	**cottage cheese**
I–2 teaspoons	**Italian seasoning**
³/₄ cup	**grated Parmesan cheese,** divided
I box	**uncooked lasagna noodles**
2 cups	**grated mozzarella cheese,** divided

Preheat oven to 375 degrees.

Stir bell pepper and spaghetti sauce into cooked sausage. Spread a large spoonful of sauce in the bottom of a 9 x 13-inch pan and set aside.

In a bowl, combine the cream cheese, cottage cheese, Italian seasoning, and ¹/₄ cup Parmesan cheese.

Place 3–4 lasagna noodles over sauce in bottom of pan. Top with half of the cheese mixture, one-third of the sauce, and ¹/₃ cup mozzarella cheese. Place 3–4 noodles on top and repeat layers. Cover with another 3–4 noodles and remaining sauce. Top with remaining cheeses.

Cover and bake 45–50 minutes; then uncover and bake 5–10 minutes more. Let stand 5–10 minutes before serving. Makes 8–10 servings.

SMOKEY PASTA BAKE

I package (25 ounces)	**meat or cheese tortellini or ravioli**
I jar (I pound, I0 ounces)	**chunky-style spaghetti sauce**
2 cups	**firmly packed spinach,** chopped
1/4 teaspoon	**red pepper**
1/4–1/2 cup	**cream or half-and-half**
6–8 ounces	**smoked Gouda,** thinly sliced

Preheat oven to 400 degrees.

Make pasta according to package directions and drain; set aside.

In a saucepan, heat the spaghetti sauce until it gently bubbles around the edges. Stir in the spinach, red pepper, and cream, and then heat through. Toss together the cooked pasta and sauce, and then pour into a 9 x 13-inch pan. Cover with cheese. Bake 15 minutes, or until it's bubbly around the edges. Makes 4–6 servings.

MAIN DISHES

CHICKEN, CHEESE, AND RICE CASSEROLE

2 cups	**wild rice**
I	**medium onion,** finely chopped
1/4 cup	**finely diced celery**
1/2 cup	**butter**
I clove	**garlic,** minced
I	**rotisserie chicken,** cut into pieces
2 cans (10.5 ounces each)	**cream of chicken soup,** condensed
I can	**milk**
2–3 cups	**grated cheese,** any kind

Preheat oven to 350 degrees.

Cook rice according to package directions. In a skillet over medium heat, cook onion and celery in butter until translucent. Add garlic and cook a few minutes more. Remove from heat and stir into cooked rice. Spread into a 9 x 13-inch pan.

Cover rice with a layer of chicken pieces. In a bowl, mix together soup and milk. Stir in cheese. Pour over chicken and rice, and bake 30 minutes until heated through. Makes 8 servings.

CHICKEN DIVAN

3–4	**boneless, skinless chicken breasts,** cut into pieces
3 cups	**broccoli florets**
I can (10.5 ounces)	**cream of chicken soup,** condensed
$^1/_2$ cup	**mayonnaise**
I teaspoon	**curry powder**
I teaspoon	**lemon juice**
I $^1/_2$–2 cups	**grated sharp cheddar cheese**

Preheat oven to 350 degrees.

Put chicken and broccoli into an 8-inch square pan that has been lightly sprayed with nonstick cooking spray.

In a bowl, mix together the soup, mayonnaise, curry powder, and lemon juice. Pour over chicken and broccoli.

Bake 30 minutes; then remove and sprinkle cheese over top. Bake 15 minutes more, or until chicken is done and cheese is bubbling. Makes 4 servings.

SWISS CHICKEN

4–6	**boneless, skinless chicken breasts**
1 container (12 ounces)	**marinara sauce**
1 package (8 ounces)	**Swiss cheese slices**

Preheat oven to 350 degrees.

Lay chicken in a 9 x 13-inch glass dish that has been sprayed with nonstick cooking spray. Cover with marinara sauce. Lay slices of Swiss cheese on top. Bake 40 minutes, or until chicken is done. Makes 4–6 servings.

ROSEMARY CHICKEN

4	**boneless, skinless chicken breasts**
I package	**Italian dressing mix**
4 tablespoons	**butter,** melted and divided
I	**small onion,** chopped
I clove	**garlic,** minced
I ½ cups	**half-and-half**
½ cup	**chicken broth**
I package (8 ounces)	**cream cheese**
½ teaspoon	**dried thyme**
2 sprigs	**fresh rosemary**
	salt and pepper, to taste

Place chicken in a 3 ½–5-quart slow cooker. Sprinkle with Italian dressing mix and 2 tablespoons melted butter. Cook on low heat 4–6 hours.

Put remaining 2 tablespoons melted butter in a saucepan and add onion and garlic. Saute until soft, then add half-and-half, chicken broth, and cream cheese. Stir until smooth. Add cream cheese mixture to slow cooker; sprinkle with thyme and fresh rosemary. Cook I hour more. Serve with mashed potatoes or noodles. Makes 4 servings.

STEAK WITH GORGONZOLA BUTTER

¹/₄ cup	**butter,** softened
¹/₄ cup	**Gorgonzola cheese**
4	**tenderloin steaks**
	Gorgonzola crumbles, to garnish, optional

In a small bowl, beat together butter and cheese until creamy. Grill steaks on a hot grill until they reach desired doneness. Top each with a dollop of cheese butter and sprinkle with extra Gorgonzola crumbles, if desired. Makes 4 servings.

SAUCY GARLIC AND BLUE CHEESE BURGERS

1 pound	**ground beef**
1/2 envelope	**dry onion soup mix**
2 cloves	**garlic,** crushed
1/4 cup	**steak sauce,** plus more
1/2 cup	**blue cheese crumbles,** plus more
4	**hamburger buns**

In a bowl, combine the ground beef, soup mix, garlic, steak sauce, and blue cheese. Form into 4 patties and then cook on a grill pan or on the barbecue until they reach desired doneness.

Put cooked patties on buns and top with more steak sauce and a sprinkle of blue cheese. Add other condiments as desired. Makes 4 servings.

JALAPEÑO TURKEY BURGERS

I pound	**ground turkey**
I	**egg**
dash	**Worcestershire sauce**
1/2	**onion,** finely chopped
1–2	**jalapeño peppers,** seeded and finely chopped
1/4 cup	**seasoned breadcrumbs**
	salt and pepper, to taste
4 slices	**pepper jack cheese**
4	**hamburger buns**

In a bowl, combine the ground turkey, egg, Worcestershire sauce, onion, jalapeño, and breadcrumbs. Season with salt and pepper. Form 4 hamburger patties and then cook on a grill pan or on the barbecue until they reach desired doneness.

When burgers are done, top each with a slice of pepper jack cheese; let cheese melt. Serve on hamburger buns with other condiments as desired. Makes 4 servings.

PROVOLONE MEATBALL SUBS

20	**frozen meatballs**
I jar (16 ounces)	**marinara sauce**
4	**hoagie buns**
I can (3.8 ounces)	**sliced olives**
8 slices	**provolone cheese**

Cook meatballs according to package directions. Place in marinara sauce in a saucepan and heat through. Once warm, place 5 meatballs on the bottom half of each hoagie bun. Sprinkle olives over top and then cover with 2 provolone slices each. Place open subs on a foil-covered baking sheet and broil until cheese is bubbling and edges of buns are slightly toasted. Makes 4 servings.

NOTE: Try cutting the meatballs in half so they don't slide around when you take a bite!

PHILLY CHEESE STEAK

1	**small onion,** sliced
1 cup	**sliced mushrooms**
1/2	**green bell pepper,** sliced
1/2	**red bell pepper,** sliced
1 container (8 ounces)	**good quality deli beef lunch meat,** cut into strips
4	**hoagie rolls**
	Cheez Whiz or provolone slices

Saute onion in oil until translucent. Add mushrooms and bell peppers, and continue to cook until desired doneness. Add meat to vegetable mixture and stir until cooked through.

Scoop mixture onto split hoagie rolls. Spread desired amount of Cheez Whiz over top half of bun and close. Meat should melt cheese, or cover meat with slices of provolone and let melt. Makes 4 servings.

FRIED CHEESE STEAKS

4 slices	**cheddar, Swiss, or provolone,** cut ³/₄ inch thick
¹/₂ cup	**flour**
1	**egg,** beaten
²/₃ cup	**breadcrumbs**
	oil, for frying

Dredge cheese slices in flour, dip in egg, and then coat with breadcrumbs. Fry in hot oil in a skillet until breadcrumbs are golden brown. Drain on paper towels and serve hot. Makes 4 servings.

CHEESE ENCHILADAS

12	**corn tortillas**
	oil, for frying
1 package (12 ounces)	**Monterey Jack cheese,** grated
2 bunches	**green onions,** sliced
1 bottle (24 ounces)	**enchilada sauce**

Preheat oven to 350 degrees.

Heat oil in a frying pan until hot but not smoking. Using tongs, quickly dip tortillas into oil, one at a time. Drain on paper towels.

Fill each tortilla with a handful of shredded cheese and a sprinkling of green onion. Roll up and place in a glass 9 x 13-inch pan that has been sprayed with nonstick cooking spray. When all enchiladas are rolled and placed in pan, cover with enchilada sauce.

Bake 20–30 minutes, or until enchiladas are hot and cheese is bubbly. Serve with Spanish rice or black beans. Makes 6 servings.

ENCHILADA CASSEROLE

1 pound	**ground turkey**
1/2 cup	**chopped onion**
3 cans (8 ounces each)	**tomato sauce**
1 1/2 teaspoons	**chili powder**
1 1/2 packages (8 ounces)	**cream cheese,** softened
10	**medium flour tortillas**
2 1/2 cups	**grated Mexican-blend cheese**
	sour cream, sliced avocado,
	olives, shredded lettuce

Preheat oven to 350 degrees.

Brown turkey in a skillet; drain fat if necessary. Add the onion, tomato sauce, and chili powder to skillet.

Spread cream cheese over tortillas, roll up, and place in a 9 x 13-inch pan that has been prepared with nonstick cooking spray. Pour beef mixture over top. Sprinkle with cheese. Cover and bake 30 minutes or until casserole is warmed through and cheese is bubbly. Garnish with sour cream, avocados, olives, and shredded lettuce. Makes 8–10 servings.

DESSERTS

STRAWBERRY CREAM CHEESE SHEET CAKE

1	**white cake mix**
1 package (8 ounces)	**cream cheese,** softened
1/2 cup	**sugar**
1 container (8 ounces)	**frozen whipped topping,** thawed
1 container	**fresh strawberries,** sliced

Make cake batter according to package directions. Spray nonstick cooking spray on a sheet pan with sides. Pour batter into pan and bake until done; let cool.

In a bowl, beat together the cream cheese and sugar. Gently fold in the whipped topping and then spread mixture over cooled cake. Place strawberry slices on top and then serve. Makes 16 servings.

SPICE CAKE WITH CREAMY FROSTING

I	**spice cake mix**
I package (8 ounces)	**cream cheese,** softened
2 tablespoons	**butter,** melted
2 tablespoons	**brown sugar**
I teaspoon	**vanilla**
I tablespoon	**honey**
$\frac{1}{3}$ cup	**chopped nuts**

Make cake batter according to package directions. Bake the cake in two 8-inch round pans; remove from oven and let cool.

In a bowl, beat together the cream cheese, butter, brown sugar, and vanilla. When the frosting starts to get thick, add the honey and beat until light and fluffy. Spread frosting over the top of one cake round and set the second round on top. Then frost the entire cake. Garnish with nuts. Makes 10 servings.

SOUR CREAM CHEESECAKE

2 cups	**graham cracker crumbs**
2 cups	**sugar,** divided
1/2 cup	**butter,** melted
3 packages (8 ounces each)	**cream cheese,** softened
3	**eggs**
1 cup	**sour cream**
1 teaspoon	**vanilla**
1 tablespoon	**lemon juice**

Preheat oven to 350 degrees.

In a medium bowl, mix together the graham cracker crumbs and 1/2 cup sugar. Mix in butter. Press into the bottom of a springform pan.

In a large bowl, cream together cream cheese and remaining sugar. Beat in eggs, one at a time. Add remaining ingredients and mix until smooth. Pour mixture over crust and bake 30–40 minutes, until the edges are dry but the center is still jiggly. Remove from oven and refrigerate for 4 hours or overnight. Makes 12 servings.

FROZEN PEPPERMINT CHEESECAKE

2 cups	**Oreo cookie crumbs**
1/4 cup	**sugar**
1/4 cup	**butter,** melted
1 package (8 ounces)	**cream cheese,** softened
1 can (14 ounces)	**sweetened condensed milk**
1–2 teaspoons	**peppermint extract**
	red food coloring
2 cups	**whipping cream,** whipped
6	**crushed peppermint candies**

In a medium bowl, mix together cookie crumbs and sugar. Mix in butter. Spray a 9-inch springform pan with nonstick cooking spray. Press crumb mixture firmly on bottom and partway up sides of prepared pan.

In a large bowl, beat cream cheese until fluffy. Gradually add sweetened condensed milk and beat until smooth. Stir in peppermint extract and food coloring; mix well. Fold in whipped cream and crushed candies. Pour filling into prepared pan. Cover and freeze 6 hours or until firm. Makes 12 servings.

LEMON CHEESECAKE BARS

2 cups	**flour**
1/2 cup	**powdered sugar**
1 cup	**butter,** softened
1 package (8 ounces)	**cream cheese,** softened
2	**eggs**
2/3 cup	**evaporated milk**
1/2 cup	**sugar**
1 tablespoon	**flour**
1 tablespoon	**lemon juice**
1 cup	**sour cream**

Preheat oven to 350 degrees.

Combine flour and powdered sugar in a medium bowl. Cut in butter with a pastry blender or two knives until crumbly. Press mixture onto the bottom and 1 inch up the sides of a 13 x 9-inch baking pan. Bake 25 minutes and remove from oven.

Put remaining ingredients except sour cream in a blender; cover and blend until smooth. Pour over partially baked crust. Bake an additional 15 minutes or until set. Cool in pan on wire rack. Spread sour cream over top and refrigerate. Cut into bars before serving. Makes 12–15 bars.

COTTAGE CHEESE RASPBERRY PIE

I container (12 ounces)	**frozen whipped topping,** thawed
I large box	**raspberry gelatin**
I container (12 ounces)	**small curd cottage cheese**
I package (8 ounces)	**frozen raspberries,** thawed
I	**graham cracker pie crust**

Mix together first 3 ingredients in a large bowl. Fold in raspberries. Pour into prepared crust and refrigerate 4 hours before serving. Makes 8 servings.

POUND CAKE WITH MASCARPONE CREAM

2 cups	**mascarpone cheese**
4 tablespoons	**sugar**
I teaspoon	**vanilla**
I	**prepared pound cake,** sliced
2 cups	**sliced fresh peaches**

In a medium bowl, beat together the mascarpone, sugar, and vanilla with an electric mixer until smooth and fluffy. Refrigerate at least I hour before serving.

To serve, top each slice of pound cake with fresh peaches and then top with a dollop of mascarpone cream. Makes 8 servings.

EASY TIRAMISU

3	**egg yolks**
1/4 cup	**sugar**
2 teaspoons	**vanilla extract**
1 cup	**mascarpone cheese**
24	**ladyfingers**
1/2 cups	**brewed coffee**
1 tablespoon	**unsweetened cocoa powder**

In a medium bowl, beat yolks with sugar and vanilla until smooth and light yellow. Fold mascarpone into the yolk mixture; set aside.

Arrange 12 ladyfingers in the bottom of an 8 x 8-inch pan. Spoon half of the cofee over the ladyfingers, and then spread half the mascarpone mixture over the coffee-soaked cookies. Repeat with remaining cookies and mascarpone. Cover and chill 1 hour. Sprinkle with cocoa powder just before serving. Makes 9 servings.

RICOTTA COOKIES

1 cup	**butter,** softened
2 cups	**sugar**
1 container (15 ounces)	**ricotta cheese**
3 teaspoons	**vanilla**
1 teaspoon	**salt**
1 teaspoon	**baking soda**
4 cups	**flour**

Glaze:

	milk, as needed
1 cup	**powdered sugar**
	decorating sprinkles

Preheat oven to 350 degrees.

In a large bowl, cream together butter and sugar. Stir in ricotta and vanilla. Sift together salt, baking soda, and flour in a separate bowl. Add dry ingredients to wet ingredients and mix until a big ball forms. Dough will be sticky.

Drop dough by teaspoonfuls onto an ungreased cookie sheet. Bake 10 minutes or until bottom of cookies are browned. Remove from oven to a wire rack to cool.

For the glaze, add milk 1 tablespoon at a time to powdered sugar until it is a nice consistency for spreading. Frost cookies and sprinkle with decorating sprinkles. Makes about 2 dozen cookies.

CHEDDAR APPLE COBBLER

I can (21 ounces)	**apple pie filling**
I cup	**flour**
$^1/_2$ cup	**rolled oats**
$^1/_4$ cup	**sugar**
I $^1/_2$ teaspoons	**baking powder**
$^1/_2$ teaspoon	**salt**
I $^1/_2$ cups	**grated sharp cheddar cheese**
$^1/_3$ cup	**butter or margarine,** melted
$^1/_4$ cup	**milk,** plus more if needed

Preheat oven to 350 degrees.

Pour pie filling into an 8 x 8-inch glass pan; set aside.

In a medium bowl, combine the flour, oats, sugar, baking powder, salt, and cheese. Stir in the melted butter and milk. If mixture is too dry, add a little more milk.

Spoon mixture over pie filling and spread evenly over top. Bake 30 minutes or until golden brown. Makes 6–8 servings.

CREAM CHEESE BROWNIES

1 package	**brownie mix**
1 package (8 ounces)	**cream cheese,** softened
1	**egg**
1/3 cup	**sugar**
1/2 teaspoon	**vanilla**
1/2 cup	**semisweet chocolate chips**

Prepare the brownie mix according to package directions. Spray a
9 x 13-inch pan with nonstick cooking spray. Spread half of brownie
batter evenly into the prepared pan; set aside.

In a large bowl, beat together the cream cheese, egg, sugar, and vanilla
with an electric mixer until smooth. Dollop the cream cheese mixture
on top of the brownie batter in pan. Top with remaining brownie
batter and swirl together using a knife or skewer. Sprinkle chocolate
chips over top.

Bake according to package directions. Brownies will be done when a
toothpick inserted into the center comes out clean. Cool in the pan,
then cut into bars and serve. Makes 12 servings.

NOTES

NOTES

NOTES

NOTES

METRIC CONVERSION CHART

Volume Measurements

U.S.	Metric
1 teaspoon	5 ml
1 tablespoon	15 ml
1/4 cup	60 ml
1/3 cup	75 ml
1/2 cup	125 ml
2/3 cup	150 ml
3/4 cup	175 ml
1 cup	250 ml

Weight Measurements

U.S.	Metric
1/2 ounce	15 g
1 ounce	30 g
3 ounces	90 g
4 ounces	115 g
8 ounces	225 g
12 ounces	350 g
1 pound	450 g
2 1/4 pounds	1 kg

Temperature Conversion

Fahrenheit	Celsius
250	120
300	150
325	160
350	180
375	190
400	200
425	220
450	230

 Check out these " 101 " favorites
for more tasty recipes:

Cake Mix	**Slow Cooker**
More Cake Mix	**More Slow Cooker**
Chocolate	**BBQ**
Gelatin	**Casserole**
Yogurt	**Dutch Oven**
Pudding	**Blender**
Mac & Cheese	**Toaster Oven**
Ramen Noodles	**Chicken**
Salad	**Rotisserie Chicken**
Zucchini	**Ground Beef**
Tofu	**Meatballs**
Tortilla	**Grits**
Canned Biscuits	**Potato**
Canned Soup	

Each 128 pages, $9.99

Available at bookstores or directly
from GIBBS SMITH
1.800.835.4993
www.gibbs-smith.com

ABOUT THE AUTHORS

Melissa Barlow is the author of five cookbooks, including *101 Things To Do With a Salad* and *101 Things To Do With Gelatin*. She is a freelance writer and editor, and lives with her husband, Todd, and their growing little family in Bountiful, Utah. Her favorite cheese is Gorgonzola.

Jennifer Adams is the author of eight books, including *Baby Showers, Wedding Showers, 101 Things To Do With Gelatin,* and *Remarkably Jane: Notable Quotations on Jane Austen*. She works as a writer and editor, and lives in Salt Lake City. Her favorite cheese is Gorgonzola.